The AWESOME Manager

The AWESOME Manager

Secrets Unveiled

Dr. Wardah Mohamad

PARTRIDGE

To order additional copies of this book, contact
Toll Free 800 101 2657 (Singapore)
Toll Free 1 800 81 7340 (Malaysia)
orders.singapore@partridgepublishing.com

www.partridgepublishing.com/singapore

CONTENTS

NOTE FROM THE AUTHOR

When I was about nine or ten, I used to follow my late dad when he went to work. Sometimes he would work in the office – this I avoided. But there were many days when he was out on site and I used to tag along. One of my fondest memories with him, was of going into a dense forest one month, and then seeing the ground cleared and a small resort being built by the sea a few months later. I saw my dad engaged in discussions, talking to his staff and leading them in projects. I saw businesses grow from scratch and watched while my dad solved numerous problems throughout the years. And I realised that one day, I wanted to do what he did.

So I enrolled in a business degree, and at the age of 21 held my first position as a manager. I have worked in many positions throughout my life, both in the business world and also in academia – and everything always comes back to management. No matter how good a product is, how much a service is demanded, how big a business grows – the sustainability of an organisation lies in how efficiently and effectively it is managed. And one thing that has caught my attention is that people without proper management background or training often find it difficult to adjust as a manager when they are promoted into the position.

This book explains the fundamentals of management from both the conventional and Islamic perspectives. Although there are some books on Islamic Management in the market, most focus on the Islamic part only and do not include the conventional theories covered in management books. The latter contain conventional principles without the Islamic perspective. This book ties the two together, making it easy for everyone to understand management from both perspectives.

When reading the book, you will realise that there are actually seven traits or behaviours that a manager should have – awareness, wisdom, empathy, sincerity, openness, morality and enthusiasm. Different words might be used but it all boils down to these seven traits and behaviour. This can be seen in the principles, examples and supporting verses of the Holy Quran – thus the title.

I dedicate the book to my late father and my husband, my idol General Managers.

A special thank you to my support team in Partridge Publishers, Reban 84, Bridesmaids, Coachies and FBM Diehards. You know who you are.….I could not have done this without you. A special thank you also to my children and siblings who have always been with me through thick and thin. And of course, my late mum, to whom I owe everything.

Read on…you are on the way to becoming an AWESOME manager!

Wardah Mohamad

CHAPTER 1

WHAT IS MANAGEMENT?

In this book, we look at management from both the Islamic and conventional perspectives, comparing between the two and coming up with how we can use management in our daily lives. The conventional perspective of management is taught in most business schools worldwide with Islamic management being taught in Islamic faculties or business schools in Islamic universities. This book offers both perspectives with a focus on how we can actually practice Islamic management in our daily business activities and daily life.

This chapter describes the meaning and functions of management and goes on to discuss the roles of managers. It will then review the main skills for managers at each level of the hierarchy.

To start off, let us look at the definition of management.

What do we understand by management? Basically, management is defined as the process of overseeing and coordinating resources efficiently and effectively in line with the goals of the organisation. Many management gurus also refer to management as getting things done through other people.

Resources refer to all resources in the organisation including the employees, the organisation's finance, physical resources such as computers and other furniture and equipment. Goals refer to the mission of the organisation and the objectives that the organisation wants to achieve.

Efficiency refers to "doing things right" i.e. are we doing things the right way? Are we minimising costs and maximising benefits?

Effectiveness refers to "doing the right thing" i.e. Are we pursuing the right goals? Are we achieving the correct targets?

We are only managing things properly if we are being both effective and efficient.

From this, we can conclude that a manager is thus someone who is directly responsible for overseeing the tasks performed by his or her employees in the organisation and is supposed to do so efficiently and effectively.

Are you a manager or aspiring to be one? Do you know anybody who is a manager? What does he or she do?

In this book, we will look at the main functions of management and the other roles that managers have to engage in.

Generally, there are five basic functions of management

Planning, organizing, staffing, leading and controlling.

Planning refers to defining the objectives to be achieved for a given period and what needs to be done to achieve the said objectives.

Organising refers to determining what tasks needs to be done, who needs to be in charge and how to do it.

Staffing refers to the recruitment of employees, looking after employees and general human resource management. Here we can include motivating and communicating with employees.

Leading involves motivating subordinates, resolving conflicts and guiding the whole organisation towards achieving the organisational goals. This relates closely to managing the culture in an organisation.

Controlling refers to the measurement of performance in all pre-determined objectives, determining the reasons for deviation and taking the appropriate actions, where necessary.

In performing his duties every day, a manager has to perform many roles. These roles were first identified by Henry Mintzberg (Mintzberg, 1973).

So what are the roles played by a manager?

Essentially, a manager plays six major roles, that of a figurehead, a leader, a liaison officer, a spokesperson, a negotiator and an initiator.

Can you give some examples of a manager playing these roles?

Let us see whether you are right….

(i) The first role of a manager is the figurehead role. A manager plays this role when he entertains clients or performs official ceremonial roles such as cutting the ribbon or declaring a function open. Attending official functions as a representative of an organisation or department is also part of this role.

(ii) The second role of a manager is that of a leader. As a leader, a manager needs to encourage and motivate his workers to work hard in order to achieve organisational goals. How does your manager motivate you? Does he give words of encouragement or gives you a pat on the back when a job is well done? What do you do as a manager? Do you encourage your staff to do their best and praise them for a job well done?

(iii) The third role of a manager is that of a liaison officer. In this role, he gives information about his unit of department to people outside the unit or outside the organisation. This can be in the form of verbal reports or even a press conference.

(iv) The fourth role is that of spokesperson. Examples of this role include a supervisor updating his operations manager on latest information or a manager lobbying local authorities with a new tender for the company. The spokesperson role is also evident when a manager represents his department or organisation in a meeting.

(v) The fifth role of a manager is that of a negotiator. A manager may negotiate salary scales with trade unions or negotiate terms of sales with a supplier. In this role, the manager often acts as a middle man between the organisation and a third party.

(vi) The final role of a manager is that of an initiator. Here, a manager initiates corporate actions and transformations which might include starting new projects, creating a good working environment or finding new ways to do something.

Now, let us see whether we can identify the roles played by the managers in the following pictures:

OPENING CEREMONY
OF NEW BUILDING

If you identified the manager speaking at the news conference as playing the role of a liaison officer – you are right!! The picture of someone giving the opening speech in a formal ceremony is an example of the figurehead role played by managers and yes, the manager in the picture is performing the negotiator role as he is discussing some issues with a colleague.

What about the skills needed by managers? There are basically three essential skills:

a. Conceptual skills – this includes decision making and analytical skills.
b. Interpersonal skills – this is the ability to communicate well and generally involves people skills.
c. Technical skills – this is basically any skill related to the job at hand e.g. typing, writing reports, and technical tasks.

Generally, technical skills are needed by lower level managers, and interpersonal and conceptual skills are needed as we go up from middle management to top level management. As a manager, you need to build up these skills to be able to do your job properly!

Let us take a break! See you in Chapter 2!

CHAPTER 2

PLANNING

In the first part of the chapter we are going to look at the definition of planning and the processes in planning. Features of smart objectives and methods of establishing commitment will also be looked at followed by the advantages and disadvantages of planning. The second part of the chapter will look at the Islamic perpective of planning.

Let us start with the definition of planning as many people use the word planning but donot really understand what it means.

Planning can be defined as setting objectives and determining ways to achieve these objectives.

What are the main processes in planning?

The first step in the planning process is to determine the objectives that need to be achieved. Then we need to build commitment from the people involved on the tasks or projects. The next step is to form action plans followed by monitoring the progress of the plan. However, there must be some flexibility throughout in case something needs to be changed, depending n the situation and circumstances.

Let us look into these processes in further detail.

How do we make sure that the objectives we set are good objectives? As a worker, we might not have any say in setting these objectives, but when we are managers, it is our duty to make sure that the objectives we set are good objectives.

The answer is simple....always make sure that the objectives are SMART...that's right S..M..A...R...T ....SMART!!

S stands for specific. This means that all objectives must be stated clearly and in specific terms e.g. A 20% increase in a profits, additional production of 50 kilograms per day or 200 in product sales.

M stands for measurable. A good objective is one that can be measured quantitatively. For example to increase student numbers by 10% every year for universities or to lose 10kgs for someone who is going on diet!

A stands for attainable or achievable - this means that any objectives set must not be impossible to achieve. Take for example, a manager asking his staff to work all through the day and night to meet production of 40 cars while he knows the maximum possible production is only 10 cars per day. This is simply unattainable!

R stands for realistic - this means that the objective must be reasonable. The example given before was both impossible and unrealistic! As managers we need to take into account not only the company objectives but the well-being of our staff as well. Asking for too much from them would just lead to stress, demotivation, and even possible injury or resignation!

T stands for timely objective i.e. a good objective must outline the time period for achievement e.g. 2 weeks, 3 months or 1 year!

So as a manager, you first need to set your department objectives based on the goals given to you by upper level management.

The second step in the planning process is one of the hardest steps for a manager to take – that of building individual commitment amongst the staff involved.

What can a manager do to gain commitment from his or her staff and encourage enthusiasm towards a certain project or plan?

One of the best ways to build commitment is through cooperation with all the staff involved. Staff will be more enthusiastic and feel more involved when they share ownership of a particular project and thus feel more responsible for it.

Next, make sure that the objectives set are reasonable. Objectives which are too high will bring pressure to the staff while objectives which are too low will result in staff being bored.

Another way to build commitment is to announce to all the staff the plan, objectives and people involved. Staff will feel committed to the project and work hard to achieve the objectives because they would be embarrassed if they fail! This may sound rather "sneaky" but it certainly works!

The last way to build commitment is to get support from upper management in terms of money, opinion or advice. This is important to pave the way for cooperation amongst all those involved.

Once commitment has been garnered from those involved in a certain plan or project, a manager has to prepare an action plan. This plan will explain in detail the steps which need to be taken, the people involved, the resources needed and the time needed for completion of a project.

The fourth step in planning is monitoring progress. In this step, a manager needs to compare between the set objectives and the actual work done. Feedback should be taken from the people involved and corrective actions taken when things do not go according to plan.

Always remember, however, that the best laid out plans may not work in real life. So, as a manager, we need to maintain some level of flexibility – make changes where necessary and be open to new ideas and new things!

Types of Plans

Now, let us look at the different types of plans that can be used by a manager:

1. Planning based on format – which includes budgets and graphics
2. Planning based on hierarchy – this includes strategic, tactical and operational plans; and
3. Planning based on frequency of use.

What are strategic plans? Basically, strategic plans are general plans that explain the overall direction of an organisation and how it should position itself in the market.

These plans are long term in nature, covering a period of 2 to 5 years and are under the responsibility of top management.

Tactical plans are prepared and implemented by middle level managers and usually explain how resources are to be used and allocated. These plans span 6 months to 2 years.

Operational plans refer to the daily planning prepared and implemented by lower level management. These plans usually explain the production and distribution of products for a period of 30 days to 6 months.

One-time usage planning refers to a specific plan prepared for a specific purpose and is only used once. An example of this would be the opening of a new business, launching of a new product etc.

Standing plans are those that are repeatedly used. These may include company policies, procedures and regulations.

The plans used by each organisation will differ depending on the size of the organisation, the nature of the business and the number of staff involved in any particular department or project. Once a plan is endorse by management, it has to be implemented accordingly. There should not be any deviation from the plan unless circumstances change. In this case, all parties involved must be informed. A contingency or back up plan should also be prepared in case problems arise during the implementation period.

From what has been explained so far, can you see why planning is important? Can you identify the advantages and disadvantages of planning?

Advantages of planning:

    a.   Generate intensive efforts
    b.   Continuous effort
    c.   Unity of direction
    d.   Establishing work strategy
    e.   Positive impact on individual and organisation

Disadvantages of planning:

    a.   Restricting changes and adaptation
    b.   Uncertainty towards assumption
    c.   Separation between planner and implementer

Did you get them right?

Now see whether you can apply the concept of planning in your daily life.

Sit down and think of what you want from your life. Have you got your plans in place? Think about it.

How long will it be before you can own your own house? Your own business? How many kids do you plan to have? How will you finance their education?

Planning in Islam:

In Islam, men's mission is to worship Allah as reflected in these verses of the Holy Quran:

(6:162-163):
Say: Truly my prayer and my service of sacrifice, my life and my death are [all] for Allah, The Cherisher of the worlds: No partner has He: This I am commanded and I am the first of those who submit to His Will.

(51:56):
"I have only created jinn and humankind so that they worship Me."

When planning, we thus need to refer to the relevant Islamic principles that govern whatever we are doing. This is explained in the Holy Quran (16:89):

"...We have sent down to we a book explaining all things, a guide, a Mercy, and glad tidings to Muslims."

We should also be prepared for contingencies and different scenarios that might happen in the course of our plans (Jabnoun: 2008).

Once something is planned, we have to implement these plans. In the course of implementation, we have to be patient and presevere no matter what comes our way. This is reflected in several verses of the Holy Quran as follows:

"Patiently then persevere. For the promise of Allah is true (40:55)."

"...Those who patiently persevere will truly receive their reward without measure (39:10)."

"But those who have been granted [true] knowledge said: Alas for we! The reward of Allah is best for those who believe and work righteousness: But this none shall attain except who steadfastly persevere [in good] (28:80)."

In the course of implementation, we also have to ensure that we do not go against any Islamic principles and do not do any bad deeds. This is explained in the Holy Quran (3:186):

"But if we persevere patiently, and guard against evil then that will be a determining factor in all affairs."

Men's mission is also to be vicegerents to Allah, as stated in the Holy Quran (6:165):

"It is He Who has made we vicegerents of the earth…"

So what does it mean to worship Allah and to be his vicegerents? Jabnoun (2008) explains this as adhering to the 5 Pillars of Islam and also all human actions in life which are undertaken to seek the pleasure of Allah. Thus, if we always remember and have it as our mission to please Allah, then all our good deeds would be counted as worship towards Allah.

The implementation of plans should also be continuous or known as *Istiqamah*. Everything should be done in stages and continuously. It is no use to rush things and fail or to do something without finishing it. This is reflected in the hadith of the Prophet Muhammad (p.b.u.h.) as reported by Ibn Majdah (Jabnun: 2008: 138):

"The best deeds are the continuous ones even if they were small in size."

Another concept related to this is is *tawakal*. *Tawakal* means that after one has planned, and executed something, for example implemented a plan, one should then pray and leave the rest up to Allah. This is reflected in the verse from the Holy Quran (29:58-59):

"….Aye… an excellent reward for those who do [good]! – Those who persevere in patience and out their trust in their Lord."

And also verse (26:217):

"And put our trust on the Exalted in Might, the Merciful."

In planning, we should make sure that our vision, mission, goals and objectives all adhere to Islamic principles and the commands of Allah. We should do only good and avoid bad deeds as all our acts will be counted and rewards or punishment given for them. As Allah explains in the Holy Quran (16:90):

"Allah commands justice, Benevolence, and liberality to kith and kin, and He forbids all shameful deeds, and injustice and transgression: He instructs you, and that you may receive admonition."

In Islam, we are bound by our long term objective of going to Heaven in the Hereafter as stated in the Holy Quran (3:185):

"Every soul shall have a taste of death and only on the Day of Judgement shall you be paid you full recompense. Only he who is saved from the fire and admitted to the Garden will have attained success: For the life of this World is but goods and catters of deception.

This is also explained in another verse (42:7):

"…And warn [them] of the Day of Assembly, of which there is no doubt: [When] some will be in the Garden and some will be in the blazing Fire."

Thus, all plans that are done should be with the purpose of entering Heaven. As Jabnoun (2008:75) states "every action a person does is directly related to the long term objective." He explains that the in Islam, emphasis should be given to this goal and not to short term or intermediate goals. Managers therefore should stress to their staff that the ultimate goal of doing anything is to worship Allah and achieve his pleasure. All our efforts and work may not be rewarded externally i.e. in terms of monetary rewards or achievements but will be rewarded in the Hereafter. Everything that we do in this life is in preparation for life in the Hereafter. Thus, everyone should be encouraged to do good and to avoid any improper conduct as everything is seen by Allah and all those who do any wrongdoing will surely be punished.

Sometimes we hear of the phrase "the end justifies the means" which means that as long as the end result is great, then how we get there is of no consequence. In Islam, this is not so. Both the means and the ends must adhere to Islamic principles and there should be no wrong doing whatsoever.

CHAPTER 3

HUMAN RESOURCE MANAGEMENT

Introduction

Human resource management is a process whereby managers will ensure the organisation has sufficient workers and qualified workers that are placed in the relevant sections and within an appropriate time, are capable of undertaking their respective tasks effectively and efficiently, as well as able to help the organisation achieve its overall objectives

Job analysis aims to identify the skills, knowledge and attitudes that are required to perform each task successfully. Job description is written statement that describes the scope of work of the employee, how the job is to be done and the purpose of carrying out the tasks given. It can be used to describe the expectations of the job to candidates. Job specification lists the minimum qualifications that an employee must have to carry out a task successfully. It can be used to draw the attention of managers to the list of qualifications necessary for an employee to carry out a task and candidates who are qualified for the task.

How can we organise for future human resource management needs? Basically, the needs of HRM should be determined by the strategic direction of the organisation. The demand for human resources depends on the demand on the products and services supplied by the organisation i.e. more staff are needed if production are increased or more staff are needed for service based companies. The overall goals of the organisation and the forecasted output provide the basis for determining the need for human resources. After the current capacity assessment and future needs analysis are done, only then can a programme be developed to match estimates with labour supply forecasts.

Once this is done, staff are recruited and we can start with the orientation, training and development.

Recruitement is the process of developing a group of candidates who are interested and qualified for a position offered by an organisation

   a. Internal recruitmen refers to any recruitment from inside the organisation
   b. External recruitment refers to any recruitement from outside the organisation

Selection of employees should follow the follow the following guidelines:

   a. Use of application forms and resumes
   b. References and background checking
   c. Selection tests – specific ability test, cognitive ability test, biographical data, personality test
   d. Interviews – either structured, semi-structured and unstructured.

What should be considered when we want to design an orientation session? Look at the figure below:

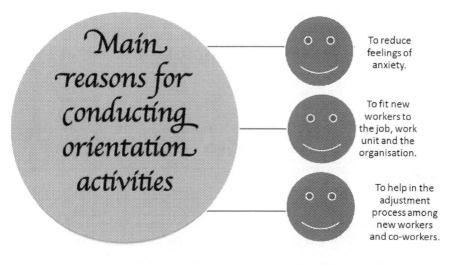

Once the staff are on board, training should also be given to them. Training needs anaylsis should be conducted which takes into account training objective and guidelines, department and organisation objectives, individual growth and performance objectives. We can then decide whether to use on-the-job training, apprentice training, off-the-job training or vestibule training.

As this is a management book, we will not discuss HRM in detail but end this section on conventional HRM by looking at the current issues in the area:

a. Diversification of employees

- Employee diversification : refers to the hiring of foreign workers, women, disabled persons,
- The recruitment process must free from discrimination.
- Applicants must feel comfortable with the organisational culture and demonstrate willingness to compromise.

b. Sexual harassment

   • Represents unsolicited sexual advances which can affect an employee's job.
   • Sexual harassment can take the form of verbal or physical harassment which will lead to an uncomfortable work environment

c. Family friendly environment

   • Family-friendly benefits are external assistance given by an organisation to the family of an employee.
   • It includes flexible working hours, leave for parents and aid for the elderly.

HRM in Islam

Islam stresses the importance of work by showing that people should work for life on earth and also for life in the Hereafter. Thus people should organise their day to achieve these objectives.

This can be seen in the following verses of the Holy Quran:

(Verse 28:77):
"But seek the abode of the Hereafter in that which Allah has given we and neglect your portion of the world…".

(Verse 62:10):
"And when the prayer is finished, then may you disperse through the land and seek of the bounty of Allah: and celebrate the praises of Allah often that you may prosper."

(Verse 9:105):
"And say: Work, soon will Allah observe your work, and His Messenger and the believers….".

And how should managers reward or compensate his employees?

The Prophet Muhammad (p.b.u.h.) explained compensation through the following hadiths (Jabnoun:2008:238-239):

"I will be against three persons on the Day of Resurrection: One who makes a covenant in my name but he proves treacherous, One who sells a free person as a slave and eats his price, and One who employs a labourer and gets the full work done by him, but does not pay him his wages" (reported by Bukhari)

"Beware, if anyone wrongs a contracting man, or diminishes his right, or forces him to work beyond his capacity, or takes from him anything without his consent, I shall plead for him on the Day of Judgement." (reported by Abu Dawud).

Managers and employers should also pay employees immediately after they have finished their work, as reflected here:

"Give a contracting man his wage before his sweat is dried." (reported by Ibn Majah).

We should also make sure that we give them what they actually deserve. This is stated in the Holy Quran (7:85):

"...Do not discredit people from what they deserve..."

CHAPTER 4

DECISION MAKING

In this chapter, we first identify the types of environment for decision making and discuss the processes involved in making rational decisions. Methods for improving decision making are looked at, along with the methods for group decision making. Finally, we look at decision making from the Islamic perspective.

The Decision Making Environment:

There are basically three types of decision making environment:

    a.   Certain conditions
    b.   Uncertain conditions
    c.   Risky conditions

Under certain conditions, we have complete information when we want to make our decision. Here, we can predict with certainty the outcome of our decision. An example of this would be when someone wants to decide between two investment decisions which have fixed returns. Since he knows the outcome of both investments, he can easily make the choice between the two.

Under uncertain conditions, we do not have any information that would help us in our decision making. Therefore, we cannot predict the outcome of our decision. People who make decisions under uncertain conditions are those who are able to take risks. For example, suppose you have just invented a new product that has never been marketed before so you do not know whether people will like your product or not. In this case, you have to take a risk if you want to sell your products as you do not have any existing information to help you.

Under risky conditions, we have some information to help us make our decision, but the information that we have is incomplete. For example, a salesman wants to sell you a diet product for losing weight. He informs you that 75% percent of his customers manage to lose weight. However, he also says that some people get sick using the product. So you can assume that if yoou buy the product, there is a 75% chance that you would lose weight. However, you do not know whether the product will work on you or would affect your health negatively. Thus you are taking a calculated risk when making your decision.

Faced with many situations and many uncertainties, how should you, as a manager make a decision?

In management, we have what is known as the rational decision making process.

Using the rational decision making process, a manager should follow the follow steps (Certo and Certo, 2016):

a. Identify the decision criteria
b. Allocate weights to each criteria
c. Generate alternatives
d. Evaluate alternatives; and then
e. Select the optimal decision

Let's say you want to buy a laptop. What would be your criteria for choosing the best one? Price? Speed? Weight?

If price is the most important criteria, then you should allocate the higher weight to this, followed by speed and weight, by order of importance.

Based on these criteria, generate some alternatives e.g. Acer, HP, Asus, Samsung.

Evaluate each brand according to price, speed and weight.

The brand that fits the most of the criteria should be the one selected!

Easy? Why not try it out in the next decision that you have to make – choosing food, buying a car or even choosing a soul mate!

A word of caution though– there are some limitations in rational decision making. As a manager, you might have limited resources so we cannot choose the optimal decision under the alternatives available. you might also find that you have too much information and therefore this complicates matters and affects your decision. You may not be able to make the best decision because you have limited access to information or the information that you have is outdated. You might not even have the necessary skills to evaluate the information available.

We have looked at individual decision making; what about group decision making?

There are three popular methods for group decision making under the conventional perspective in management (Certo and Certo, 2016):

a. Brainstorming
b. Nominal group technique
c. Delphi technique

Brainstorming is a group decision making process in which negative feedback is forbidden until all alternatives have been heard by all members involved in the brainstorming process. Under this method, group members share ideas while the group leader records each idea where the group can read it. These ideas will all be evaluated once all the ideas are recorded. The best idea will be chosen once the advantages and disadvantages are have been considered. Organisations often use brainstorming to get new ideas from employees or to find solutions to current issues in the workplace.

Under the Nominal group technique, each group member writes down individual ideas on the decision or problem and then each member presents individual ideas orally. These ideas are usually written down on the whiteboard or mahjong paper. The entire group discusses ideas simultaneously. When the discussion is completed, a secret vote is taken to allow members to vote without fear. The idea which receives the most votes is adopted and implemented.

Under the Delphi Technique, a problem is identified and group members are asked to give solutions by providing responses to a carefully designed questionnaire. Using this method, group members do not have to meet face to face and responses are compiled and sent out to all members. Individual group members are then asked to generate a new individual solution to the problem. These steps are repeated until consensus is reached. This technique is often used by organisations to get ideas or solutions from professionals in their respected fields.

Now, take a minute and try to think of the advantages and disadvantages of group decision making.

Did you manage to come up with these advantages?

Advantages of group decision making:

a. Sharing of experience and skills among group members
b. More information, data and facts can be compiled
c. Problems can be seen from various perspectives
d. Increases acceptance and commitment of members on the decision made

Did you come up with these disadvantages?

Disadvantages:

  a. Time consuming
  b. Discussion might be controlled by certain individuals
  c. Have to compromise
  d. High costs involved if many group members have to meet
  e. Pressure to agree with group decision
  f. Groupthink (compromising on quality of decision to maintain relationships in a group)

Decision Making in Islam

In Islam, a manager should not make decisions alone but should make decisions after consultation with his peers and subordinates. This is called *Shura* (Jabnoun, 2008) and is explained in the Holy Quran (42:38) as follows:

"Those who hearken to their Lord and establish regular prayer; who [conduct] their affairs by mutual consultation; who spend out of what We bestow on them for sustenance."

The Prophet Muhammad (p.b.u.h) was reminded of this by Allah in the verse (3:159):

"It was by the mercy of Allah that we were lenient with them (O Muhammad), for if we had been stern and fierce of heart they would have dispersed from all round about you. So pardon them and ask forgiveness for them and consult with them upon the conduct of affairs. And when we are resolved then put our trust in Allah. Lo! Allah loves those who out their trust [in Him]."

Jabnoun (2008) explains that Shura is aimed at building consensus that will be of benefit to the people making the decision. In the case of no consensus, we should ask the team members to vote as advised by the Prophet Muhammad (p.b.u.h.):

"My nation cannot agree upon an error and if a conflict persists be with the majority." (reported by Ibn Majah in Jabnoun: 2008).

Conclusion:

When we compare decision making in the conventional perspective and the Islamic perspective, we can summise that both are applicable and are more or less the same in the sense that we need to take into account the facts and circumstances which surround a particular problem before making a decision. Whenever possible, we should consult the people around us to ask for their opinions and discuss things before making a decision. However, there are times, when as a leader, we have to make the decision ourselves, and subordinates have to follow, as shown in the case of the battle of Uhud where the Prophet Muhammad (p.b.u.h) gave strict instructions to his followers but they failed to follow his orders. This resulted in them losing the battle.

Before we finish for this chapter, let me leave you with a game to play with your friends or family to test your decision making skills:

Assume that you are all on a boat and that the boat is sinking. You have 1 minute to decide who can go on the emergency raft which fits 2 people and who are to be left behind!

Enjoy yourselves, and remember, if you cannot decide in 1 minute....

See you in Chapter 5!

CHAPTER FIVE

MOTIVATION

In this chapter we will first describe what is motivation and explain how motivation works according to two models of motivation. Then we will discuss motivation from the Islamic perspective.

What do we know of motivation?

Definition of motivation

Motivation can be described as consisting of powers that are able to move, direct and enable a person to be diligent in their effort to achieve goals. I like to think of motivation simply as an inner force which propels us to achieve our goals.

Look at the following diagram on motivation:

Needs are physical and psychological requirements that have to be fulfilled in order to ensure our existence and wellbeing e.g. food, shelter etc. Values are developed over our lifetime and may differ from person to person. Goals will also differ from person to person and can change over time.

Motivation can be divided into intrinsic and extrinsic motivation. Intrinsic motivation refers to our internal thoughts and feelings which propel us to do something. This would include confidence, self-esteem and the need for success. For example – you might have a desire to obtain a higher degree in order to gain more knowledge or you might have a compulsion to excel in everything that you do.

Extrinsic motivation refers to things or situations around us that encourage us to do something. Kids for example, might be motivated to study if we give them toys as a reward; employees always look forward to getting bonuses when they have done a good job!

Stop and think – what are your intrinsic and extrinsic motivators?

Approaches to Motivation:

There are two basic approaches to motivation (Certo and Certo, 2016):
- Need-based models which emphasise the specific needs of humans or internal factors that give power to direct or stop action; and
- Process-based models which focus on the understanding of thinking or the cognitive process that exist in the mind of the individual and actions that affect the behaviour of an individual.

Here, one need based model and one process based model will be discussed.

Let us look at Maslow's Model of Hierarchical Needs, a need-based model, first

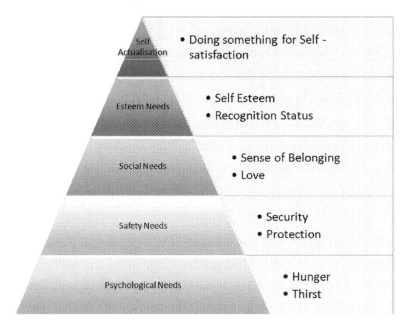

From the above, we can see that there are basically five level of needs. Physiological needs are needs such as thirst, hunger and shelter. These are basic needs. An organisation can motivate workers by giving them salaries that would enable them to obtain, food, water and housing. They can also motivate workers by providing them with a comfortable working environment such as flexible work hours, air-conditioned rooms and a pantry with basic amenities such as fridges and microwaves.

Safety needs are needs related to a safe physical and emotional environment. An organisation which offers health insurance and retirement benefits are able to motivate their workers to stay with the organisation as they fulfill the workers' safety needs. Would we leave an organisation which offers full medical coverage for another which does not provide any? If the pay was the same or only slightly higher, most people would certainly think twice!

Social needs include the need for friendship, love and the feeling of belonging. Social needs are fulfilled when workers have many friends in the workplace and feel that they are a part of the organisation. As a manager, we thus need to make sure that we have a conducive and friendly work environment and culture so that our staff are happy to come to work everyday.

Esteem needs refer to the need for status and recognition. People need to know that the organisation appreciates their work and recognize their contribution. Organisations can fulfill this need by paying bonuses according to performance, announcing best employees of the month and celebrating achievements with workers through family days and award recognition.

Self-actualisation needs are the highest needs in Maslow's hierarchy. People who have these needs value high achievement based on their own capability and potential. At this stage, workers value their own self-satisfaction over other needs such as high pay or recognition. They want to do the best that they can and work to fulfill their own work satisfaction. These workers will only stay with an organisation when they have exciting jobs and tasks that fulfill their expectations. Rewards such as money or other benefits might not motivate them anymore.

Maslow believed that once a lower need is fulfilled, we will start to fulfill higher level needs and so on.

Equity Model of Motivation:

Employee's Self		Comparison to Other People	Perception
Reward / Input	=	Reward / Input	Equality
Reward / Input	<	Reward / Input	Inequality
Reward / Input	>	Reward / Input	Inequality

Accoarding to this model, the existence of inequality can result in pressure equivalent to the level of inequality felt by the employee resulting in reduced input, demand for increased income or resignation (Certo and Certo, 2016).

Motivation is Islam:

We know now that motivation is whatever it takes to propel us to achieve our goals.

One of the things that employees appreciate is praise. Although all work should be done for the sake of Allah and there should be sincerity in the job, praise is a form of recognition that can motivate people. This is reflected in the Holy Quran (14:24-26):

"See you not how Allah sets forth a parable? A goodly word like a goodly tree whose root is firmly fixed, and its branches reach the heavens. It brings forth its fruits at all times by the leave of its Lord. So Allah sets forth parables for people in order that they may receive admonition. And the parable of an evil word is that of any evil tree: it is torn up by the root from the surface of the earth. It has no stability."

And in verse (2:83):
"…And speak to people Good…"

As a manager and a leader, we should always reward our employees and followers in order to motivate them. This is shown in the Holy Quran (18:30):

".....We never waste the reward of anyone who did good."

We should also differentiate between those who do good and those who do not as people would be demotivated if those who do bad also get rewards. Furthermore, as a manager, we should encourage those who have made mistakes to correct themselves and do good, as reflected in (11:114):

".....For those deeds that are good remove those deeds that are evil..."

What happens when things are tough and we feel down and demotivated? According to conventional theories as explained above, we should find things that would help us to motivate ourselves, whether it be material things, acknowledgment, friendship or for those who are at the top of Maslow's hierarchy, the feeling of self-satisfaction is enough for doing something.

In Islam, the goal is always getting to Heaven thus whatever we do, motivate ourselves by knowing that even if things are not going well now, things will be better in the Hereafter as long as we are doing what Allah tells us to do. When we are feeling sad or something has gone wrong, motivate ourselves by knowing that everything happens according to Allah's will. When we face obstacles in life and feel burdened, remember that Allah is testing us and that He will not test beyond what we are capable of. This is explained in the Holy Quran (2:286):

"On no soul does Allah place a burden greated than it can bear...".

In another verse (65:7) it is explained that everyone should spend within his means and that Allah puts no responsibility on anyone over than what has been given to him:

"Let the man of means spend according to his means: and the man whose resources are restricted, let him spend according to what Allah has given him. Allah puts no burden on any person beyond what He has given him. After a difficulty Allah will soon grant relief."

This verse clearly shows that Allah will grant relief and give reward if one is patient enough in facing the challenges and difficulties facing him or her.

Thus we should be patient and always be grateful for what we have. We should be motivated to do our work **sincerely** whether it be at home or in the office. We should do everything because of Allah. Be happy no matter what as everything happens for a reason and we should wholeheartedly embrace whatever comes our way as Allah certainly knows best what is for us.

This is clearly explained in the Holy Quran (45:13):

"And He has subjected to we, as from Him all that is in the heavens and on the earth: behold, in that are signs indeed for those who reflect."

And

(47:7):
"O we who believe, If we help [the cause of] Allah, He will help We."

Finally, no matter what happens in the workplace, one is advised to work hard for the sake of Allah and fight against feeling frustration and hopelessness (Ahmad, 2006) for we should always remember that the main reward bestowed on us will be in the Hereafter. As Allah reminds us in the Holy Quran (28:77):

"But seek, with the wealth which Allah has bestowed on we, the Home of the Hereafter. Nor forget thy position in this world, but do good as God has been good to we and seek not occasions for mischief in the land, for God loves not those who do mischief."

My advice:

Set your goals high and don't stop till you get there…Stay motivated always!

And of course…

Never, never, give up! Allah is always there for us.

CHAPTER SIX

COMMUNICATION

In this chapter, we will look at the importance of communication in an organisation and differentiate between formal communication and informal communication. We will then look at the forms of communication and how to overcome barriers to communication. We then end the chapter with the Islamic perspective to communication.

Let us start with the definition of communication. Communication is the process of transferring information and knowledge from one party to another using meaningful symbols. It is a method of exchanging and sharing of ideas, attitudes, values, opinions and information.

How does communication take place?

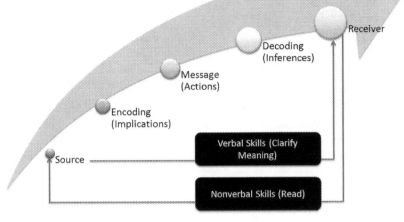

From the diagram above we can see that communication begins with the sender and ends with the receiver. Here, the sender is the source of the message. Encoding happens when the sender translates information into a series of symbols that can be identified and understood by the receiver. These symbols can be in the form of verbal, written or sign language and is known as the message.

Channel is the mode or method of delivery. This can be a conversation, a letter, e-mail, memo, a video or even physical gestures. Now, we can add social media to the mix where a lot of communication is done via Facebook, watsapp and other applications. The process whereby the receiver translates the message received is known as decoding. The receiver translates the message into a form that can be understood and brings meaning to him. Feedback is the reaction of the receiver towards the message. The receiver gives this feedback to the sender of the message. Sometimes, there are things or occurrences which disrupt, confuse or restrict the message sent. This is called noise.

Did you talk or write to anyone today? Can you relate your experience with the process shown in the diagram above?

Now let us go on to the three main types of communication – formal, informal and grapevine.

Formal communication can be vertical (either upwards or downwards), horizontal or diagonal. This may include letters, e-mails and memos sent within staff members in the organisation or meetings and discussions.

Informal communication is known as the grapevine. Examples of informal communication include people talking over lunch or communicating on a personal basis via on-line applications. Though some people regard the grapevine as rumours, it can be a useful source of information for both staff and management and many successful organisations use the grapevine as an important communication tool.

The last type of communication is non-verbal communication. This type of communication does not use words, either verbal or written. Kinesics is an example of non-verbal communication. Here, people communicate using body language and facial expressions.

Can you guess what the people in the photos are communicating? Are they angry or happy or entranced??

Paralanguage is another example of non-verbal communication where the sender communicates his message using tone, pitch, intonation, level or silence.

Hmmm…let's try this out.

"Alright, boss, I will do it." (happy tone)

"Alright, boss, I will do it!" (angry tone)

Can you guess the feelings behind the two messages? Even though the message is the same, the first one shows that the staff is happy to do the job while the second one shows that the staff is upset. As managers, we should learn to read the meanings behind our employees' messages. As employees, we should certainly learn to see when our boss is happy or angry!!

Most people assume that once a message is sent, it will be received without any problems and that the receiver will surely understand what we mean. Unfortunately, this is not always the case. Often, there are barriers to effective communication and these can be in the form of selective perception, disruption, emotions, communications skills and suspicion.

Selective perception is the tendency to listen and process information which is consistent with our own values, beliefs and desires and ignore anything which is inconsistent with them. For example, if you like football, you would probably listen and absorb any facts about football but simply turn a deaf ear when someone is talking about dancing or yoga!

Disruption can be any factor that interrupts, confuses or restricts communication. This can be any type of noise or even static over the telephone! Even a hot environment in a meeting room can be a disruption as people in the meeting will tend to miss parts of the messages sent in the meeting because they are not comfortable.

Emotions can also influence the message sent and message received. Anger, love, hate, jealousy or fear can often lead to misunderstandings. For example, if somebody you like praises you, you would feel good. However if somebody whom you do not like and whom you know does not like you praises you, you might start thinking "Now, what is she up to?"

Communication skills could also be a barrier to communication. Languages, and the level of understanding might be different, thus resulting in mixed messages and understanding. Suspicion could also act as a barrier to communication. Workers are often suspicious of management as they often fear reprimands or maybe even layoffs when the economy is bad. This might lead to misunderstandings and negative behaviour. A manager who is always suspicious of employees tend to control them and act overbearing, which will certainly put employees of and result in an unhappy work environment.

So, are there any ways to overcome communication barriers and thus improve communication? Of course, there are!

First, control the flow of information. As managers, you must know the level of our staff's understanding and send them information according to the level that they are capable of receiving. Do NOT give too much information at one time.

Secondly, encourage feedback. Always ask for your staff's opinion and ask for their input. Never, ever, look down on them. They can be sources of ideas and inspiration!

Take care with the language used. Make sure people understand the language that you are using. Do not speak English if your staff can only understand Malay and vice versa! The message would not be understood!

Listening actively and pay attention to body language. You might be surprised with what you learn! Also control negative emotions – no matter how angry or upset you feel, do not let it show. Stay calm and listen until you finish sending or receiving the full message. You can also use non-verbal signs – nodding your head when you approve of something and smiling as a show of appreciation.

Lastly, use the grapevine when necessary. Sometimes, employees are too afraid to tell you up front if they have problems or are feeling unhappy. Listen to them – as managers, you must be informed at all times.

Communication is important, as without communication, the organisation will cease to exist.

Communication in Islam:

It was reported by Bukhari as reported by Anas (Imam Az-Zabidi, 2014) that whenever the Prophet (p.b.u.h.) said something, he usually repeated it three times so that it would be understood, and when he asked for permission to enter a house, he repeated the salam three times. This shows that in Islam, a message needs to be repeated and iterated, to make sure that is conveyed properly and fully understood.

Allah says in the Quran, "He has taught him to talk (and understand)" (Qur'ān 55:4). Prophet Muhammad (peace and blessings of Allah be to him) used both written and oral communication. For example, he memorised the Quran and made sure that his followers memorised the verses too. The prophet also used written communication in conveying instructions and sending messages. Syed Kazim (2013) gave the example of written communication by the Prophet - a letter to Ashamah bin Al-Abjar – then king of Abyssinia (now Ethiopia), a letter to Juraij bin Matta (Muqawqis) – then king of Egypt, a letter to Chosroes – then emperor of Persia, a letter to Heraclius – then emperor of Byzantium, a letter to Mundhir bin Sawa – then governor of Bahrain, a letter to Haudhah bin Ali – then governor of Yamamah, a letter to Al-Harith bin Abi Shimr Al-Ghassani – then king of Damascus and a letter to Abd bin Al-Julandai and his brother Jaifer who was the king of Oman.

Syed Kazim (2013) also cited the recording of the Quran in written form including tablets, bones, animal skins and date palms. The Quran was later compiled in book form by Caliph Abu Bakar after the passing of the Prophet (p.b.u.h). The Quran has been preserved for over 14 centuries and nothing in it has been changed. It is an excellent example of written communication and how it has been used as a guide, as a source of knowledge and as a rule book on the way we Muslims should live.

Another form of written communication that Islam has deemed compulsory is the recording of financial transactions or debts. It is stated in the Holy Quran (2:282)

> *"O you who have believed, when you contract a debt for a specified term, write it down. And let a scribe write (it) between you in justice. Let no*

scribe refuse to write as Allah has taught him. So let him write and let the one who has the obligation (i.e., the debtor) dictate. And let him fear Allah, his Lord, and not leave anything out of it. (Qur'ān 2:282).

It is also stated in the Holy Quran (41:33):

"And who is better in speech than one who invites to Allah and does righteousness and says, 'Indeed, I am of the Muslims'." (Qur'ān 41:33).

This verse shows that Allah places a great importance on speech and promises that the best speakers are those who invites people to believe in Him and Islam.

By Afifa Jabeen | Arab News | 10 Jun 2012

Afifa Jabeen (2012) gave an excellent example of the Prophet's communication skills. She cited this story of the Jews who used to insult and provoke the Prophet (p.b.u.h) by saying, *"Al-saam 'alaikum (Death be upon you),"* while he would continue to be gentle with them, while only replying: *"And upon you too."* The Prophet's wife, Aisyah (p.b.u.h) could not bear it and so she said *"And death be upon you too, and Allah's curse and anger!"* The Prophet (p.b.u.h) said: *"Take it easy O'Ayesha! You should be gentle. You shouldn't curse or be harsh."* She said, *"Didn't you hear what they said?"* He said, *"Didn't you hear what I said? I prayed against them and that prayer will be accepted, whereas their prayer against me will not be accepted."*

The Prophet was indeed exemplary in his communication, always being positive and soft spoken to everyone, even his enemies. He portrayed the best behavior and communicated well, thus earning respect from others. Stories of people converting to Islam due to how he communicated with them abound and each of these stories show how important communication is in Islam.

Afifa Jabeen (2012) further pointed out that the nature of the Prophet's speech differed when he talked with different people. For example, he would talk about expeditions and weapons with Abu Bakr (May Allah be pleased with him), while he would involve his wife Aisyah in jokes and cheerful talk. Further, the Prophet's (p.b.u.h) good manners extended to everyone. He displayed the best form of treatment with children. Whenever he visited the Ansar, he would greet the children and place his hand on their heads out of compassion. He would always try to make the people happy with his speech.

This shows that when we communicate, we should tailor our communication to the receivers of our message whether in the content, the language used and the tone of voice.

The Messenger of Allah (p.b.u.h) also displayed the best of interpersonal and mass communication skills, which were evident from the gatherings he held with his companions. His message would be loud and clear, ensuring the message is correctly received. Moreover, when the Prophet (p.b.u.h.) noticed a person making a mistake, he would not confront him directly to preserve him from humiliation. Instead he would say, *"What is wrong with the people who do such and such?"* The Prophet (p.b.u.h) never criticized as reported by Anas (may Allah be pleased with him), who served the Prophet for nine years.

The Prophet (p.b.u.h) said, *"Let a man come to the people how he likes the people to come to him,"* meaning treat the people how you like to be treated by them. So as managers, we should communicate well with our employees and treat them as how we want to be treated. Never shout at them and never humiliate them. Always be courteous.

You can better your speech and improve your relationships by reciting the dua that Prophet Musa (p.b.u.h) recited when Allah SWT sent him to the Pharaoh (Afifa Jabeen, 2012):

"O my Lord! Open for me my chest. And ease my task for me; And loosen the knot from my tongue. That they understand my speech." (The Holy Quran 20: 25-28)

CHAPTER SEVEN

LEADERSHIP AND CULTURE

In this chapter, we will look at leadership and culture; and differentiate between a manager and a leader. We will then compare various theories of leadership and discuss contemporary leadership styles. We will conclude with the Islamic perspective on leadership.

What is Leadership?

What is leadership? Leadership is a process of influencing other people to achieve group or organisational goals. Who then, are leaders? Are managers also leaders? Let us look at each one in turn.

Managers are generally very efficient people and manage the status quo. They study the processes in the organisation and make sure these processes run smoothly. They manage any problems that arise and are known as problem solvers. They execute the commands given by top management, and more often than not, look at matters in the short run.

Leaders, on the other hand look at effectiveness in the organisation. Where managers do things the right way, leaders actually look to see whether they are doing the right thing. They do not just execute orders but look at the outcome and the future. Leaders promote change, inspire people and motivate them.

Thus, we can say that a manager may be a leader, and a leader can be a manager, but usually they have different personalities and outlook as shown above.

Approaches to Leadership

There are three main approaches to leadership – the leader-centred approach, follower-centred approach and interactive approach.

The Leader-centred approach focuses on the personality features or traits of leaders such as physical form and behaviour and includes studies by Ohio State University, Michigan University, Blake and Mouton's managerial grid and studies on leadership styles (Certo and Certo, 2016). Studies by Ohio State University look at the consideration and structural behaviour of leaders.

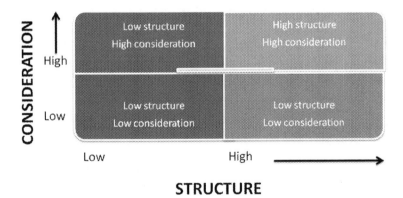

Consideration behaviour refer to feelings of consideration towards employees while structural behaviour refers to behaviour of forming the work procedures of subordinates. The study found that leaders with a high level of consideration are more inclined to have satisfied subordinates compared to leaders with a low level of consideration. Leaders who have a high level of structural behaviour but are low in terms of consideration will face a high frequency of complaints and resignation among employees.

Another study is the Michigan study, which identified the basic principles that contribute towards group productivity and satisfaction. In this study, consideration and structural behaviour are exclusive and at the opposite sides of a continuum. Leaders who are inclined towards feelings of consideration must reduce structural behaviour and vice versa.

Blake and Mouton's managerial grid classified the styles of leader management according to their managerial grid where there are 5 types of leaders – country club management, team management, middle of the road, impoverished leadership and authoritarian as shown in the diagram (Bateman and Snell, 2013). They suggested that the team management is the best as these leaders have both high consideration towards employees and high consideration towards products. Country club management leaders have high consideration for employees but low consideration for products while authoritarian leaders are just the opposite. Middle of the road leaders are moderate leaders while impoverished leaders are the weakest as they do not care about either employees or production!

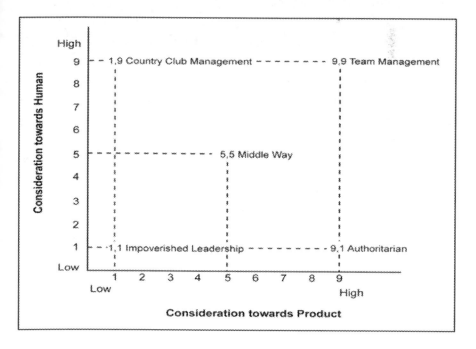

The last approach to leader centred leadership divides leadership into three types of styles- autocratic leaders, laisser faire leaders and democratic leaders. Autocratic leaders make decisions for the whole group. Laissez-faire leaders allow members of the group to make all the decisions while democratic leaders guide and encourage the group to make decisions.

Which leaders are we? Telling people what they want to hear or taking people where they need to be?

Under the Follower-centred approach, self-leadership is a paradigm for creating leaders who are ready to lead themselves. Under this approach, variables such as employees, tasks, and features can make it difficult for leaders to influence followers or cause them to be unnecessary.

Another approach to leadership is the interactive approach which includes the:

- Situational model
- Fiedler's contingency model
- Path-goal model; and
- Leader behaviour model

The situational model was developed by Paul Hersey and Kenneth Blanchard (Certo and Certo, 2016). This model is based on the assumption that leadership styles should portray the maturity level of subordinates. Using the quadrants shown, leaders should decide whether to facilitate, coach, delegate or direct their employees.

Fiedler's Contingency Model was introduced by Fiedler and looked at the favourableness between a leader's personality features with situational conditions as shown in the slide. This model focused on three dimensions of leaders – leader-subordinate relations, task structure and position power.

Leader - member relation	Task Structure	Position power	Situation	
Good	High	Strong	I	Favourable
Good	High	Weak	II	
Good	Low	Strong	III	Intermediate
Good	Low	Weak	IV	
Poor	High	Strong	V	
Poor	High	Weak	VI	Unfavourable
Poor	Low	Strong	VII	

The Path-goal model was introduced by Martin Evans and Robert House (Certo and Certo, 2016). They stated that a leader is able to increase the satisfaction and performance of subordinates by setting the path towards achievement of goals by increasing rewards

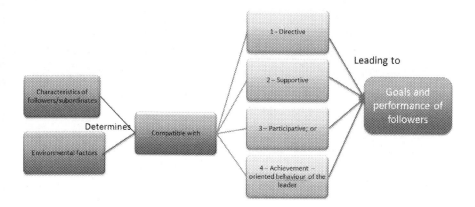

Types of leadership under Path-Goal model include (Yukl, 2013):

- Directive – which focuses on rules, regulations, standards
- Supportive – which allows employees to be close
- Participative – where the leader holds discussion to obtain views and inputs
- Achievement oriented – where the leader sets challenging goals and standards

The Continuum of leader behaviour was introduced by Tannenbaum and Schmidt (Bateman and Snell, 2013) and proposed that Different situations required different leadership styles. Leadership style would depend on forces within the leader, forces within subordinates and forces within the situation.

Under Strategic Leadership, there are four types of leaders:

- Visionary – leaders who create positive images for the future
- Charismatic – leaders with high levels of reference force
- Transactional – leaders who favour punishment and rewards
- Transformational – leaders who are able to motivate employees beyond their own needs and instead look at the group's needs

Let us look at some examples of leaders….

As a leader we should spread enthusiasm, inspire confidence and demonstrate integrity. Create a sense of urgency, lend the team our energy and make things fun! Keep our employees informed, seek their advice and convince them to try new things. Remember, our team is always watching us – make sure that what they see is what they will get…lead by example. Do the right thing always…

Some leaders like to tell people to do things but they themselves do nothing….

Some leaders create paths that people will follow....

What about us?

As a leader, we need to be strong, as the responsibility of our followers or our employees lie on our shoulder. It is not an easy task, and not every manager can be a great leader. But as a manager, we really need to try...

Leadership and Culture in Islam

What are the traits of a leader according to Islam?

Allah tells us that the best of men to employ is one that is strong and **honest**, as stated in the Holy Quran (28:26):

"Truly the best of men for we to employ is the [man] who is strong and **trustworthy**."

A good leader should also be **kind** and **caring**. This is stated in the Holy Quran (3:159

"It was by mercy of Allah that we were lenient with them [O Muhammad], for if we had been stern and fierce of heart they would have dispersed from round about we. So pardon them and ask forgiveness for them and consult with them upon the conduct of affairs. And when we are resolved, then put wer trust in Allah. Lo! Allah loves those who put their trust [in Him]."

A leader should also be just and fair. This is clearly stated in the Holy Quran (16:90):

"Allah commands justice, benevolence, and liberality to kith and kin, and He forbids all shameful deeds, and injustice and transgression: He instructs us, that we may receive admonition."

And verse (5:8):

"O we who believe! Stand out firmly for Allah, as witnesses to fair dealings and not hatred of others to we make we swerve to wrong and depart from justice. Ne just that is next to piety....".

A leader should also be **aware** of followers' potentials and limitations so that he is able to harnass those potentials and further develop his followers. The prophet Muhammad (p.b.u.h.) stated as reported by Muslim:

"Whoever said, people are in loss is either the most lost among them or one who caused them to be loss."

Allah also states patience and resolve as characteristics of a leader. This is seen in these verses of the Holy Quran:

(3:186):

"...But if we persevere patiently, and guard against evil then that will be a determining factor in all affairs."

(46:35):

Therefore patiently persevere, as did the messengers of inflexible will...."

Leaders should also be knowledgeable and possess great **wisdom** as they need to manage others and make important decisions. This can be found in the Holy Quran (28:14):

"When he [Musa] reached full age, and was firmly established [in life], We bestowed upon him **wisdom** and knowledge: for this do We reward those who do good."

Another important trait of a leader is being a good example to his followers. A good leader must lead by example and teach their followers how to do tasks instead of simply giving them instructions. This will instill commitment in the employees and team members as they know that the leader also does work and actually knows what he is doing! Being able to show a good example is a very good way of influencing followers to do what we want them to do.

Allah states this in the Holy Quran (61:2-3):

"O you who believe! Why say we that which we do not? Grievously odious is it in the sight of Allah that we say that which we do not."

Allah also reminds us in verse (2:44):

"Do we enjoin right conduct on people and forget (to practice it) ourselves…."

Prophet Muhammad (p.b.u.h) was the ultimate leader and messenger of Allah and Allah tells us to follow in his footsteps and imitate his character. This is shown in the Holy Quran (33:21):

"Verily in the Messenger of Allah we have a good example for him who looks unto Allah and the Last Day, and remembers Allah much."

Another characteristic that a leader should have is forbearance. This is shown in the Holy Quran (11:75):

"For Abraham was, without doubt, forebearing, compassionate and given to look for Allah."

This is further iterated in verse (32:24):

"And we made, from among them, leaders [a'immah], giving guidance under our command, so long as they display patience [sabr], and continue to have firm faith [yaqin] in our signs."

Jabnoun (2008:209) describes this:

"Leaders should not take things personally and react out of anger or in response to provocation. They should always keep a big heart that transcends egos. They shall keep their composure, their rationality and their **wisdom**."

A leader should also be good at communicating as the way a leader speaks enables him to impart knowledge and influence his followers. The story of Musa in the Holy Quran (28:34) reflects this:

"My brother Harun [Aaron] is more eloquent in speech than I: so send him with me as a helper, to confirm [and strengthen] me: For I fear that they may accuse me of falsehood.

A leader should also be always be willing to learn and continuously build his knowledge. This is important as a leader leads his followers and a knowledgeable team is essential for success, especially in the current fast paced global environment. The willingness to learn is stated in the Holy Quran (20:114):

"….And say: "O my Lord! Increase me in knowledge…".

Ahmad (2006:77) suggested that a Muslim corporate culture should be based on the following:

(a) *Tawheed* and its implications on man, that is, in terms of viewing work as a set of worship (*Ibadah*) and an approach to the rebuilding of Islam.
(b) Islamic brotherhood
(c) Islamic social guidelines, such as no backbiting, no spreading of rumour and evils.
(d) Islamic enhancement of the skills of the employees in terms of training and upgrading of knowledge.

Syed Othman et al (1998) recommended the following values be inculcated in an effort to promote an Islamic Corporate Culture:

(a) Every action should be based on a stated intention
(b) Conscientousness and knowledge to be utilized in all endeavours.

Let us look at the culture of the Companions of the Prophet (p.b.u.h.). Jabnoun (2008) explained the culture that formed the basis for their success:

(a) Tawhid – the belief in One God which is Allah. This belief is from the Holy Quran (112:1-4) which states:

"Say: He is Allah, the One and Only, Allah the Eternal, Absolute, He begets not, Nor is He begotten. And there is none like unto Him."

How did this relate to the Companions' success? Their belief in Allah the AlMighty gave them the confidence to do what is right and to fear no one but Allah, thus freeing them of following any other rules but those of their God.

(b) Unity of Purpose:

The Companions also had unity of purpose – that of serving Allah. This is important as if we do something with the intention of serving and pleasing Allah, this is considered as Ibadah or worship. Thus, even if we work to achieve organisational goals, the end goal should be to please Allah as men's purpose in life is to secure Allah's blessings and reward in the Hereafter. This is clearly stated in the Holy Quran (33:4):

"Allah has not made for any man two hearts in his body."

Thus, everything that we do should be because of Allah.

(c) Belief in the Hereafter and reward and punishment:

Another value that the Companions held on to was the complete belief in the Hereafter. They steadfastly believed that everything that we do on Earth will be rewarded or punished in the Hereafter, thus they would be held accountable by Allah in everything that they do. This encouraged them to do only good and avoid evil behavious. This is based on the verse from the Holy Quran (2:136):

"Say We: We believe in Allah, and the revelations given to us and to Abraham, Ismaelm Isac, Jacob, and the tribes, and that given to Moses and Jesus, and that given to [all] prophets from their Lord. We make no difference between one and another of them and We [bow and submit] to Allah."

(a) Independence:

Independence here refers to independence from tyranny and the dictate of others. For example, a manager who practices independence would take the initiative of solving problems without getting directions from top management. The same manager would also be strong enough to say no if management asked them to do something which is against the rules of Islam as they are not afraid of anyone but Allah.

As stated in the Holy Quran (17:30):

"Verily your Lord does provide sustenance in abundance for whom He pleases, and He provides in a just measure, for He does know and regard all His servants."

This value of independence is further explained in the Holy Quran (65: 2-3):

"...And for those who fear Allah, He (ever) prepares a way out, and He provides for him from (sources) he never could image."

  (b) Responsibility and Accountability:

Another value that was held strongly by the Companions was that of responsibility and accountability. They were always responsible in leading their people and were always accountable for what they did. Thus, we should not pass blame to others. As leaders, we should be responsible for our followers and fully accountable for not only our actions, but for theirs as well.

The Prophet (p.b.u.h) stated (Al-Bukhari):

"Behold! Each one of we is a guardian, and each one of we will be asked about his subjects. A leader is a guardian over the people and he will be asked about his subjects; a man is a guardian over the members of his household; a woman is guardian over the members of the household of the husband and of his children...Behold! Each one of we is a guardian and each one of we will be asked about his subjects."

  (c) Participation:

The Companions also practised participation through consultation and advice as consultation is mandatory in Islam. Here, participation is in the form of Shura' which is an exercise taken to achieve consensus. Should consensus not be achieved, then we should follow the majority. This is in line with the Prophet's advice (Ibnu Majdah):

"My nation cannot agree upon an error and if a conflict persists be with the majority."

As a Muslim, we should always do good and forbid what is wrong. This is stated clearly by the Prophet (p.b.u.h.) as reported by Muslim:

"Whoever see wrong, should correct it."

This is also stated in the Holy Quran (3:104):

"Let there arise out of we a band of people inviting to all that is good, enjoining what is right, and forbidding what is wrong or evil."

(d) Justice:

The Companions also practised justice in all that they did. This is important to ensure that everyone is treated fairly and employees are happy in doing their job. This value is clearly reflected in the Holy Quran (16:90):

"Allah commands justice, benevolence, and liberality to kith and kin, and He forbids all shameful deeds, and injustice and transgression: He instructs us, that we may receive admonition."

The importance of justice can also be seen from the Hadith from the Prophet Muhammad (p.b.u.h) as reported by Bukhari from Abu Hurairah r.a. (Al-Hafiz Al-Munziri: 2013) which explains that a leader is like a shield. He will be made an enemy from behind and feared in front. When he commands his people to believe in Allah and he is just, then he will receive reward. But if he commands otherwise, he will surely receive the punishment which is commensurate with his commands.

(e) Dignity, respect and privacy:

Three values that are important in Islam include dignity, respect and privacy which are reflected in these two verses from the Holy Quran:

(17:70):

"We have honoured the children of Adam, provided them with transport on the land and the sea, given them for sustenance things good and pure and conferred on them special favours above a great part of Our Creation,"

(49:12):

"O we who believe, avoid suspicion as much (as possible) for suspicion in some cases is a sin and spy not on each other...."

Thus, we have to behave with dignity and always respect others. We should also respect other people's privacy and avoid suspicion as much as possible.

(f) Trust:

The Companions also considered trust as a very important value. There must be trust between leaders and followers and also among followers. This is based on the Prophet's (p.b.u.h.) hadith reported by Abu Dawud:

"A leader who is suspicious of his people will lead them to mischief."

(g) Time Efficiency:

Another value practised by the Companions was that of time efficiency. This is very important because as Muslims, we know that this life is in preparation for the Hereafter. Thus, time should not be wasted, as seen by the Companions' life which was nearly always full and was a continous jihad (struggle).

As stated by the Prophet (p.b.u.h.) and reported by Tirmidhi:

"Take advantage of five before five: Our youth before our aging, our health before our sickness, our wealth before our poverty, our free time before our busy time and our life before our death."

And

"Take advantage of five before five: Wer weth before wer aging, wer health before wer sickness, wer wealth before wer poverty, wer free time before wer busy time and wer life before wer death."

(h) Caring and Sharing:

The Companions practised the culture of sharing and caring where they existed as one and could feel the pain of one another. There was always a sense of collectiveness and they cared for each other. This follows from the Prophet's (p.b.u.h) saying as reported by Bukhari:

"The believers are like one man, if his head is in pain, his whole body suffers and if his eye is in pain his whole body suffers"

and

"None among we will believe until he loves for his brother what he loves for himself."

(i) Eagerness to learn:

One of the most important values held by the Companions was their quest for knowledge. They were very eager to learn as this is what Allah has told us to do in the Holy Quran (97: 1-5):

"Read! In the name of our Lord and our Cherisher, Who created – created man, out of a mere clot of blood: Read! And our Lord is Most Beautiful – He who taught with the pen – taught man what which he knew not."

This quest for knowledge is also reflected in the Prophet's statement as reported by Ibn Majah:

"Seeking knowledge is a must for every Muslim – male and female."

Why is being a good leader so important? If everyone understood it, there would be no abuse of power in organisations. When one assumes duty as a manager, one assumes leadership over one's employees and as such are responsible for them. As a leader, we then become accountable for those who are working under us. This was explained by the Prophet Muhammad (p.b.u.h) as reported by Bukhari (Jabnoun:2008: 160; Al-Hafiz Al-Munziri, 2013):

"Behold! Each one of we is a guardian, and each one of we will be asked about his subjects. A leader is a guardian over the people and he will be asked about his subjects; a man is a guardian over the members of his household and he will be asked about his subjects; a woman is guardian over the members of the household of the husband and of his children....Behold! Each of we is a guardian and each of we will be asked about his subjects."

Conclusion

Conventional leadership shows us the different types of leaders we can be and the different styles that we can adopt. Although all these are readily seen in the organisation, we need to be the right kind of leader – someone who leads by doing the right thing and adheres to Allah's will, someone like the great Prophet (p.b.u.h.) and his companions.

Chapter Eight

MANAGING TEAMS

Introduction

In this chapter, we will look at the differences between groups and teams; and then identify the advantages and disadvantages of teams. Following this, we will distinguish amongst the different types of teams and discuss the factors involved in building high performance teams. The chapter will conclude with a discussion on teamwork in Islam.

Groups and Teams

Is there a difference between groups and teams? Some people use the terms interchangeably but actually, there is a difference between the two. A group consists of two or more individuals who interact and are independent of each other towards achieving a certain objective. A work group is a group that shares information and makes decisions in order to assist its members to perform their jobs well in a relevant field. Performance is assessed based on individual contribution to the group. A team on the other hand is an interdependent and complementary entity in all aspects with a commitment to achieve the same goals. Performance in teams is assessed based on team achievement

Can you identify which groups are teams and which are not?

Organisations nowadays like to use teams in their bid to achieve their goals and complete required tasks. What are the advantages and disadvantages of using teams?

By using teams, an organisation can:

   a. Enhance customers' satisfaction
   b. Increase the quality of products and services; and
   c. Increase the levels of job satisfaction

However, there are also disadvantages of using teams:

   a. high turnover where the members of a team may change at any point of time.
   b. social loafing where some team members do not put all their effort in the team and instead act as sleeping partners.
   c. the behaviour of self-restriction is also a disadvantage where a team member does not seem to have any views or do not take part in team discussions or tasks.

So when should management use teams? Basically there are five general situations where teams should be used. A team should be used when the objectives of a certain task or project is clear. A team should also be used when tasks cannot be done individually. Teams can also be used when rewards provided are for team performance and many resources are available. Lastly, teams can or should be used when there is clear authority in managing and modifying work methods.

Are all teams the same or are there different types of teams to be used for different situations? Basically, there are 7 different types of teams that managers can use:

   (a) Employee involvement team
   (b) Semi-autonomous team
   (c) Self-managed team
   (d) Self-designed team
   (e) Cross-functional team

(f) Virtual team; and

(g) Project team

An employee involvement team provides ideas and advice to management but does not have power to make decisions. Meetings for this type of team are held periodically during office hours. Issues discussed include occupational safety and health issues, customer relations and quality of products. Meetings to discuss sales and marketing are also under this type of team.

A semi-autonomous team has authority to make decisions and solve problems relating to main tasks of product and service productions. However, using this team, management still plays a role, although a lesser one compared to traditional work groups.

A self-managed team manages and controls the overall main tasks in the production of products and services. Generally, it can do anything related to production without waiting for instructions from management. This might include teams in factory production or maybe the production team for a bakery.

A self-designed team possess the characteristics of a self-managed team but differs in that it also controls the design of the team, work activities and team memberships.

A cross-functional team consists of employees from different fields or functions in the organisation. The members of a cross-functional team can be either part-time, temporary or permanent. An example may be a special team set up for a specific project where the members consist of members from the functional units in the organisation including staff from marketing, finance, research and the like.

A virtual team exists when members are in different geographical areas or organisations and uses telecommunications and information technology to carry out activities. Team members in this virtual team do not meet face to face. These teams can be utilized for special projects and they carry out all discussions and tasks using emails and other on line media.

The last type of team is the project team, which is formed to carry out a task or project in a particular time period. This team is led by a project manager who has full responsibility for planning, membership and team management.

Let us now look at the characteristics of teams:

a. Team norms are informal rules or standards which are agreed upon in order to control the behaviour of team members.
b. Team unity refers to how far team members are attracted to becoming members of the team and are motivated to stay permanently in the team
c. Team conflict refers to fighting over limited resources, arguments and discrepancy in opinions.

The question thus arises on how we can build high performance teams:

First, make sure that the size of the team is suitable with the task given. Take only capable team members and provide role models for team members. Do not forget to promote diversification! The team leader should make sure that the members are committed towards the same purpose and are set to build specific goals. There should also be a suitable performance and reward system so that members are motivated and achieve satisfaction with the work done. Lastly, develop absolute beliefs where each member absolutely believes that the success of the team can only be achieved with the contribution of each team member.

Teamwork in Islam

Islam holds teamwork as very important. This can be seen from the following verse of the Holy Quran (3:103):

"And hold fast together, to the rope of Allah and do not be divided...".

In relation to this, Allah reminds us that we must always respect one another and not speak or think bad of another, as reflected in this verse (49: 11-12):

"O you who believe! Let not some men among we deride others: It might be that they [the latter] are better than them [the former]. Nor let some women deride other women: It may be that the latter are better than the [former]: Nor defame nor be sarcastic to each other nor call each other by [offensive] nicknames: Ill-seeming is a name connoting weaknesses, [to be used by one] after he has believed; And those who do not desist are [indeed] doing wrong. O we who believe avoid suspicion as much [as possible]: for suspicion in some cases a sin: And spy not on one another, nor speak ill of one another behind their backs. Would anyone of we like to eat the flesh of his dead brother? Nay, we would abhor it... But fear Allah: For Allah is Oft-Returning, Most Merciful."

Conclusion

Teamwork is very important and every manager should be well versed in the selection of team members and the building of high performance teams. I will leave you with this simple activity for building teamwork in the organisation:

1. Divide the participants into three groups.
2. Ask each team to find a musical clip to represent their team style or personality. The music may reflect that the team is shy, stormy, indifferent, aggressive, icy, adventurous, romantic.
3. Play the clips in front of everyone and ask the other teams what they perceive the team represents.
4. Then the actual group members explain to everyone why they chose the music clip and what they represent.

CHAPTER NINE

CONTROL

Introduction

In this chapter, we discuss what is controlling and why we need control in the organisation. We then look at the steps in the control process and the different forms of control. We then conclude with controlling from the Islamic perspective.

People often associate the word control with the act of controlling someone or something. In this picture, the man is trying to control the elves by catching them! Controlling in management refers to a systematic effort to fix or establish the standard of performance through planning objectives, designing information feedback systems, comparing true performance with fixed standards and generally ensuring that organisational activities are running according to plan.

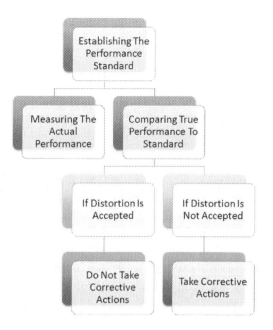

In essence, controlling involves asking and answering the questions of:

a. Where we are? .ie. measuring our current performance
b. Where we planned to be? i.e. looking back at what we planned to achieve
c. How can we get back on track i.e. what steps can be taken to ensure that we achieve the targeted performance.

How can we implement control? Is it as simple as pressing the buttons on the remote like we control our channel selection?

Unfortunately, things are not always that easy!

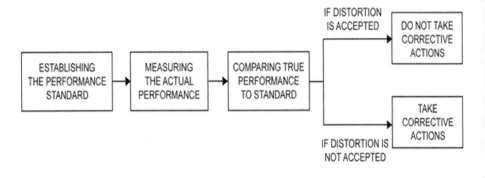

The control process starts by setting the standards for performance. Once a particular task or project is done, the actual performance should be measured. The actual performance should then be compared to the set standards. If there is any variation, we, as the manager should decide whether the variation should be accepted. If it cannot be accepted, corrective actions must be taken to bridge the gap.

Now, let us look at the basic methods of control.

Future control or pre-control refers to control before a problem takes place. This means that a manager should predict future problems so that preventive actions can be taken to avoid the predicted problems. Concurrent control refers to managing problems when it happens while feedback control refers to managing problems after is has happened.

What about the forms of control?

Basically, there are five forms of control:

    a.   Bureaucratic control
    b.   Objective control
    c.   Normative control
    d.   Concertive control; and
    e.   Self control

Bureaucratic control uses the hierarchy to control employees i.e. control via the formal position in an organisation. Rewards are given to those who obey orders while punishment is given to those who do not obey orders.

Objective control uses the measurement of observation towards the behaviour of employees or output produced to evaluate work performance. There are two forms of objective control which are behaviour control and output control.

Behaviour control is the rule of behaviour and actions that control behaviour of employees. Output control controls the output of employees through rewards and incentives; for example more rewards for more outputs produced.

Normative control is control through norms and beliefs shared together among all members in the organisation. In other words, the organisational culture is used to control employees in an organisation.

Concertive control is normally used in an autonomous work group. It uses norms and behaviour which have been discussed, formed and agreed to by the members of the group as a control mechanism.

Self-control refers to a situation where managers and employees control their own behaviour by establishing their own goals, monitor their own progress and their own achievements and reward themselves.

Look at the picture…do we sometimes feel like this and want to shout in frustration??

We have looked at the purpose of control, the steps involved and the forms of control. But what do we, as managers need to control?

Generally, managers need to control the following factors in order for the organisation to achieve its goals:

a. Finance
b. Human resources
c. Internal Operations; and
d. Customers

For example, as a manager we need to draw up budgets for wer department and decide how much we want to spend on each project or job. We also need to control our human resources – their attendance, their performance and their compensation. The internal operations of the organisation can be further controlled by measuring the quality of processes and products. Finally, a manager has to control his customers by making sure that the retention rate is high and that they are satisfied with the services and products of the company!

Control in Islam:

Control is actually very simple in Islam. If we believe in Allah and the hereafter, we know that we are going to be rewarded and punished based on what we do. Thus there is really no need to have other forms of control.

As stated in the Holy Quran (16:97):

"Whosoever does good, whether male or female, and he is a believer, We will most certainly make him live a happy life, and We will most certainly give them their reward for the best of what they did."

Another form of control is in the form of contracts where Islam dictates that future obligations should be written in the form of a contract. This is shown in the Holy Quran (2:282):

"O you who believe! When we deal with each other, in transactions involving future obligation in a fixed period of time, reduce them to writing. Let a scribe write down faithfully as between the parties; let not the scribe refuse to write: as Allah has taught him, so let him write. Let him who incurs liability dictate, but let him fear his Load Allah and nor diminish aught of what he owes. If the party liable is mentally deficient, weak, if if he were not able to dictate, let his guardian dictate faithfully. And get two weaknesses out of wer own men. And if there are not two men, then a man and two women such as we choose, for witnesses so that if one of them errs, the other can remind her…".

Self-control is also evident in Islam as Allah tells us repeatedly to control ourselves from doing bad or shameful deeds. This is reflected in the following verses of the Holy Quran:

(Verse 16: 90):

"Allah commands justice, the doing of good, and liberality to kith and kin and He forbids all shameful deeds, injustice and rebellion: He instructs us, that we may receive admonition."

(Verse 5:8):

"O we who believe! Stand our firmly for Allah, as witnesses to fair dealing, and let not the hatred of others to we make we swerve to wrong and depart from jsutice. Be just, that is next to piety."

Control is indeed important as reflected in this verse in verse (2:251) of the Holy Quran:

"…Did not Allah check one set of people by means of another, the earth would indeed be full of mischief…".

In terms of financial control, we are reminded to pay zakat (alms) and also to offer charity in order to cleanse the income that we make.

In verse (64:15-16) of the Holy Quran, Allah tells us:

"And they have been commanded no more than this: to worship Allah, offering Him **sincere** devotion, being true in faith. To establish regular prayer and to give zakat. And this is the religion right and straight."

Zakat is used to bridge the gap between the rich and the poor whereby those who earn a certain amount if money and other riches including silver and gold, are required to give away a percentage of this to the poor. In this way, the poor will be able to meet their daily needs and the rich are controlled so as not to overspend or indulge in extreme and extravagant spending.

The Prophet Muhammad (p.b.u.h.) also reminded us to give charity and reminded us that "nobody's assets are reduced by charity" (Ahmad, 2006).

So what have we learnt today? Try and recall….

As a student, as a human being, what do we think of control? How can we use it in our daily life?

Chapter 10

CONCLUSION

As a manager, we are accountable and responsible for what we do and what our employees do. We are blessed with what Allah has given us and it is up to us how we manage this and the people under us. As stated in the Holy Quran 2:29):

"He it is Who has created for we all that is on the earth…."

And

(67:15):

"It is He who has made the earth obedient and manageable for us, so we traverse through its tracts and enjoy the sustenance which He furnishes: but unto Him is the resurrection."

We need to continuously learn and better ourselves so that we can be the leader that is required of us; we should also stay humble as we are here to serve Allah and worship Him. We are here on the earth for a purpose, and we should be full responsible for what we do.

As Allah states in the Holy Quran (16:78):

"It is He who brought we forth from the wombs of our mothers when we knew nothing; and He gave we hearing and sight and intelligence and affections: that we may give thanks [to God]."

Let us be the best of managers and manage the people in our team as best as we can, because of Allah and with the help of Allah…

Holy Quran (47:7):

O we who believe, If we help [the cause of] Allah, He will help us….

As managers and leaders, and as employees and followers, let us manage our lives properly and achieve success, both in this world and in the hereafter.

Let us pray to Allah, the most Benevolent, the most Merciful:

The Holy Quran (2:201):

"And of them [also] is he who says: Our Lord! Give us in the world that which is good and in the Hereafter that which is good, and Guard us from the doom of fire."

In all the principles covered and also in the verses of the Holy Quran, seven main traits and behaviours stand out:

Awareness
Wisdom
Empathy
Sincerity
Openness
Morality
Enthusiasm

As a manager, we should be aware of everyone around us and the environment that we work in. If there is something wrong, it is our responsibility to fix it. We should always keep on learning as we need our wisdom to move forward. We should also have empathy for our employees because without them, nothing will get done. Appreciate what they do. Be sincere in our work and always remember that we are but vicegerents of Allah. We should also be open – open to people, open to ideas, open to criticisms and open to change. And despite all challenges, all opportunities, we should always maintain our morality and adhere to the commands of Allah. Lastly, but not least, we should be enthusiastic as we are managing other people. It is our enthusiasm that will spur people forward...

Be AWESOME!!

BIBLIOGRAPHY

Afifa Jabeen (2012) Arab News, 10 June, http://islam.ru/en/content/story/prophet-communication-role-model

Ahmad, K. (2006) Management from Islamic Perspective, Research Centre, International Islamic University Malaysia, Kuala Lumpur.

Certo, S.C. and Certo, S.T. (2016) Modern Management, 14th ed, Upper Saddle River, New Jersey: Pearson Education Inc.

Jabnoun, N. (2008) Islam and Management, International Islamic Publishing House, 2nd edition, Riyadh.

Imam Az-Zabidi (2014) Ringkasan Sahih Bukhari, Jilid 1, Al-Hidayah Publication, Kuala Lumpur

Al-Hafiz Al-Munziri (2013) Ringkasan Sahih Muslim, Jilid 2, Al-Hidayah Publication, Kuala Lumpur.

Syed Kazim (2013) at http://www.radianceweekly.com/350/10284/sayedee039s-conviction--a-travesty-of-justice/2013-03-17/communication/story-detail/the-concept-of-communication-in-islam.html

Syed Othman Alhabsi, Syed Omar Syed AGil, Nik Mustapha Nik Hassan, Aidit Ghazali (1998) Islamic Management for Excellence, Kuala Lumpur: INMIND.

Mintzberg, H. (1973). The Nature of Managerial Work, New York: Harper & Row.

Bateman, T.S. and Snell, S.A. (2013) Management (10th ed.), New York: McGraw Hill.